Little Leaders

BOLD WOMEN
IN
BLACK HISTORY

Little Leaders

BOLD WOMEN

IN

BLACK HISTORY

VASHTI HARRISON

PUFFIN

PUFFIN BOOKS

UK | USA | Canada | Ireland | Australia
India | New Zealand | South Africa

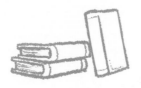

Puffin Books is part of the Penguin Random House group of companies
whose addresses can be found at global.penguinrandomhouse.com.
www.penguin.co.uk   www.puffin.co.uk   www.ladybird.co.uk

Penguin
Random House
UK

First published in the USA by Little, Brown 2017
Revised edition published in Great Britain by Puffin Books 2018
This edition published 2019
001

Printed in Italy

A CIP catalogue record for this book is available from the British Library

ISBN: 978–0–241–34684–6

All correspondence to:
Puffin Books, Penguin Random House Children's, 80 Strand, London WC2R 0RL

MIX
Paper from
responsible sources
FSC
www.fsc.org   FSC® C018179

QUOTE SOURCES

10   '. . . never lost a passenger': Harriet Tubman at a women's suffrage convention, New York, 1896.

21   'Colour is life': Alma Woodsey Thomas in Josephine Withers, *Women Artists in Washington Collections* (University of Maryland Art Gallery and Women's Caucus for Art, 1979).

25   'I made up my mind to try. I tried and I was successful': From an interview with Bessie Coleman, 'Aviatrix Must Sign Life Away to Learn Trade', *Chicago Defender*, 8 October, 1921.

43   'I am the candidate of the people': From Shirley Chisholm's presidential campaign announcement speech on 25 January, 1972. Her full sentence was 'I am the candidate of the people of America'.

46   All Maya Angelou quotes from Maya Angelou, *And Still I Rise* (Random House, 1978).

64   '. . . would make others feel the history': From an interview with Octavia E. Butler in *Publishers Weekly,* included in her obituary in the *New York Times*, 1 March, 2006.

TO ALL THE WOMEN

WHOSE STORIES ARE IN THIS BOOK:

THANK YOU FOR BEING LEADERS,

THANK YOU FOR BEING BRAVE,

THANK YOU FOR BEING BOLD.

WE ARE GRATEFUL AND WE ARE INSPIRED.

TO ALL THE LEADERS YET TO COME, BIG OR LITTLE:

I CANNOT WAIT TO HEAR YOUR STORIES.

Contents

Mary Prince
Circa 1788 - Circa 1833

AUTHOR, ABOLITIONIST

Born into slavery in Bermuda, Mary was very rarely in charge of her own story. In the course of her life she was bought and sold five times, separated from her family and forced into gruelling, back-breaking work. For her first forty years she was powerless in a system that saw her only as property. Any rebellion would result in beatings, floggings or worse. Only when her master was away on business did Mary act in defiance: she learned to read and earned some of her own money. In 1826 she met and married a free man, but when her owners found out, she was severely beaten.

In 1828 she travelled to England with her owners, but swiftly escaped to freedom. Slavery was banned in Britain but was still legal in the colonies. So, although Mary was free, there was no way she could travel back to her husband. Instead she took action and began to campaign for the abolition of slavery throughout the British Empire.

In 1831 she wrote and published her autobiography, *The History of Mary Prince, a West Indian Slave, Related by Herself,* the first account of the life of a black woman ever published in Britain. In this shocking and impactful book she recalled the awful brutalites of her upbringing. Through her detailed storytelling she helped people realize just how terrible it was to be a slave in the colonies. The book was so successful it printed three times that year.

Finally, in 1833, the Slavery Abolition Act was passed and slavery was outlawed throughout the British Empire! Mary used her story and her powerful words to reach people and, in turn, to help change history.

Seaman William Brown
circa 1794 – ?

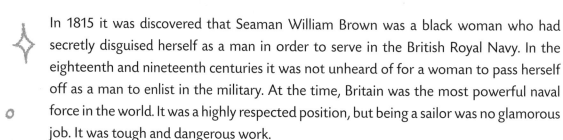

SAILOR

In 1815 it was discovered that Seaman William Brown was a black woman who had secretly disguised herself as a man in order to serve in the British Royal Navy. In the eighteenth and nineteenth centuries it was not unheard of for a woman to pass herself off as a man to enlist in the military. At the time, Britain was the most powerful naval force in the world. It was a highly respected position, but being a sailor was no glamorous job. It was tough and dangerous work.

There are a few varying accounts of William Brown's story. One version was published in the *Annual Register* for 1815. It states that she served on the flagship of Britain's premier battle fleet, the HMS *Queen Charlotte*, for upwards of eleven years! The story says she took on many jobs aboard the ship and was capable of steering the wheel and navigating through shallow waters. She even served for some time as captain of the fore-top: leading the other sailors high above the ship in the upper sails.

An official document from the ship – the muster list – tells a different story. It states that on 23 May 1815 a twenty-one-year-old man from Grenada joined the crew of the HMS *Queen Charlotte* as a landsman – the lowest-ranking crew member – and was discharged on 19 June, for 'being a female'. If that is the true story of William, she served for twenty-seven days, which was no easy feat. As a landsman she was entirely new to the hard work of life at sea and had to keep her identity a secret.

We may never know exactly what happened to William Brown, and we do not know her true name, but one thing is clear: she successfully enlisted and served her country and is recorded as the first black female to serve in the British Navy.

Sojourner Truth
Circa 1797–1883

ABOLITIONIST, WOMEN'S RIGHTS ADVOCATE

Sojourner was born a slave in New York state under the name Isabella Baumfree. Following the state's Gradual Emancipation Act, she was due her freedom in 1827. When she realized that her owner was planning to keep her enslaved, Sojourner ran away with her infant daughter in tow. But this came at a huge cost. She had to leave behind her five-year-old son.

The slave owner sold Sojourner's son to a plantation a thousand miles away in Alabama. Meanwhile Sojourner remained in hiding in New York until her freedom was official. When the coast was clear, she brought a court case, saying that her son had been sold illegally. She was one of the first black women to bring a court case in America, and even though it seemed impossible, she won. She got her son back!

In 1843 she changed her name to Sojourner (which means traveller) and became a preacher. She travelled the country, sharing her messages for women's rights and the abolition of slavery everywhere. Although Sojourner could neither read nor write, her voice carried far. In December 1851 she gave a speech that she made up on the spot. In it she spoke up on behalf of black women who faced the double discrimination of racism and sexism and had often been left out of the fight for equality. The speech is known by its most famous refrain: 'Ain't I a Woman?'

She went on to encourage African Americans to fight on behalf of the Union in the American Civil War, for former slaves to be given places to live, and for desegregation of streetcars (trams). She was an agitator and a fierce activist for equality.

"Ain't I a Woman?"

Mary Seacole
1805 – 1881

NURSE, ENTREPRENEUR

Mary was born in the British colony of Jamaica to a Scottish father and Jamaican mother. From an early age she learned nursing and healing from her mother, who used traditional remedies and kept a boarding house for invalid soldiers.

As a young woman, Mary explored the Caribbean, visiting Cuba, Haiti and the Bahamas all on her own – a bold and unusual step, especially for a woman of colour. She also travelled with her husband, Edwin Seacole, who died after only eight years of marriage. Mary continued to explore Central America and then Britain, and along the way she picked up new medicine techniques. She combined her knowledge of traditional herbal nursing with modern European methods.

In 1853 a war began along the Crimean Peninsula in Eastern Europe. It was a conflict between the Russian Empire and the allied British, French and Ottoman Empires. Mary wanted to enlist as a military nurse to help the wounded, but her application to the British War Office was refused. She did not let that stop her. She travelled to the Crimean Peninsula with a friend and set up a hotel and boarding house – the British Hotel – behind enemy lines. She used her savvy business skills to provide hot food, drinks and clothes for wounded soldiers. Mary bravely nursed soldiers on the battlefield as well as in the British Hotel. Her dedication to the servicemen was unmistakable – she formed a strong bond with the soldiers she helped. Many years later, when she faced financial troubles many of them banded together to raise money for her.

In 1857 she released *Wonderful Adventures of Mrs Seacole in Many Lands*. On 30 June 2016 a statue of her was unveiled at St Thomas's Hospital in London, honouring her as a pioneer in her field. She is remembered as a brave and fearless leader!

Harriet Tubman
1822–1913

ABOLITIONIST, NURSE, SCOUT, SPY

One of nine children, Harriet was born into slavery under the name Araminta Harriet Ross. Both her parents were West Africans, from the Ashanti warrior people. While many of her siblings were sold and traded to distant plantations, one good fortune Harriet managed was to remain with her parents throughout her youth. When she was fifteen, Harriet was accidentally hit in the head with an iron weight, and fell into a coma for three days. Her brain injury resulted in narcolepsy – a permanent disorder that caused her to fall asleep at random times. Fearing her slave owner would eventually discover her injury, she decided to run away to avoid the risk of being sold or traded.

After escaping from the Confederate South in 1849, Harriet could have stayed in the North (where slavery was outlawed). But knowing it was possible to escape, she wanted to return for her family and anyone else she could rescue. Over eleven years she returned to the South thirteen times and led more than seventy men, women, and children to freedom and safety via the secret system called the Underground Railroad. Known as a 'conductor', she 'never lost a passenger' on her journeys. Even though it was dangerous, she continually put her life at risk for others. Later, during the American Civil War she served as an army nurse and went undercover as a spy for the North.

Harriet was always looking to help other people. What very little she had she gave away to others. She lived in poverty for most of her life and donated her time, money and property to those in need.

In 2016 the US Treasury announced a historic proposal to change the $20 bill: it would replace the face of President Andrew Jackson with Harriet, making her the first woman on the front of any American paper currency.

Rebecca Lee Crumpler
1831 – 1895

PHYSICIAN

From the very beginning, caring for others was a part of Rebecca's life. She was raised in Pennsylvania by her aunt, who provided healthcare services to the people in her neighbourhood. Helping her community became her passion and her life's mission.

She attended a private school in Massachusetts and went on to work as a nurse for eight years. In 1860 she applied to an all-white medical school, the New England Female Medical College – a bold and risky move, but she was accepted. Rebecca graduated in 1864, becoming the first African American woman doctor in the country. Out of more than fifty thousand physicians in the United States at the time, only about three hundred were women, and Rebecca was the only black woman.

She began her practice in Boston, specializing in the care of women and children. But when the Civil War came to an end, she moved to Richmond, Virginia, to work with the Freedmen's Bureau. The fallen Confederate South was extremely hostile to the newly freed slaves, so Rebecca worked with the bureau to provide healthcare to them. Rebecca had been born free in Delaware – the state with the highest number of free black people before the war. She was new to the adversity and racism of the South, but she endured it in order to help the poor and needy.

Throughout her career, Rebecca was concerned with the health of women and children. In 1883 she published a two-part text entitled *A Book of Medical Discourses*. The first part focuses on care for infants and the second part on women's health. It is possibly the first medical article published by a black woman.

Mary Bowser
Circa 1840 – ?

CIVIL WAR SPY

Very little is recorded about Mary's life. What we do know is that she was born into slavery in Richmond, Virginia, around 1840. She was purchased by the wealthy Van Lew family as a companion for their daughter, Elizabeth. The Van Lews were no ordinary family in the Confederate South, though. They had a secret: they were spies for the free Northern (Unionist) states, and abolitionists involved in the secret Underground Railroad.

Before the Civil War, when Mary was still in her teens, Elizabeth granted her freedom and arranged for her to receive an education in Philadelphia. Mary wanted to assist the Van Lews in their efforts against the Confederacy. At that time in the South, it was illegal for a black person to be educated or even to learn to read. For this reason, no one would ever suspect that Mary was a threat. As a slave, she could hide in plain sight. So she agreed to go undercover as a slave in the house of Jefferson Davis, the Confederate (Southern) President. While cleaning, she would steal glances at confidential memos, and while serving dinner she would eavesdrop on conversations between Confederate officials. She passed information about troop movements and army plans to Elizabeth, who passed them along to Union officials. Rumour has it that Mary had a photographic memory and was able to read a page once and recite it back word for word.

After the war Mary educated freed slaves and travelled around the United States, giving speeches. For a long time she was careful to conceal her true identity, using a variety of aliases. Eventually she disappeared completely, but she is remembered. In 1995, she was inducted into the American Military Intelligence Hall of Fame.

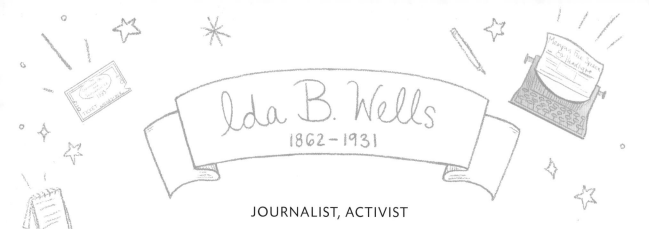

Ida B. Wells
1862 – 1931

JOURNALIST, ACTIVIST

Ida was a natural-born activist. Wherever she saw injustice she stood up against it. She was born a slave in Mississippi, but emancipation came to the South when she was still a child, and this meant she had the opportunity to get an education. After college she worked as a teacher but lost her job for criticizing the poor conditions in black segregated schools.

In 1884, seventy-one years before Rosa Parks refused to give up her seat on a bus in Montgomery, Alabama, Ida refused to leave her seat in the women's carriage on a train in Memphis, Tennessee. She had purchased a first-class ticket but was asked to leave and join the African-American carriage.

Ida did not go quietly.

She brought a legal case against the railway company and eventually won it: there was no rule that said black women could not ride in the 'women's' carriage. However, laws allowing segregation soon appeared in Tennessee, and Ida's case was overturned. Afterwards she wrote a newspaper article about the incident, under the name Iola. Later she became known as Iola, Princess of the Press.

Journalism became her outlet. She was the co-owner and editor of the *Memphis Free Speech and Headlight* and later the *Free Speech*. She took a strong stance against lynching and faced death threats for her words. In 1898 she led a huge anti-lynching campaign all the way to the White House. Ida knew the power of words and knowledge, and continued to use her voice to stand up for what was right.

Memphis Free Speech and Headlight

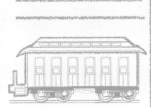

"Iola, Princess of the Press"

"The way to right wrongs is to turn the light of truth upon them."

Stop LYNCHING NOW!

Down with LYNCHING

END LYNCHING.

STOP LYNCHING NOW!

Zora Neale Hurston
1891 – 1960

WRITER, FOLKLORIST, ANTHROPOLOGIST

Zora's unique upbringing led her down a path of storytelling and creativity. She was raised in Eatonville, a historic town in northern Florida. Eatonville was special because in 1886 it became the first self-governed, all-black city in America. It was an idyllic, nurturing environment that fostered an extreme sense of pride in its culture and traditions.

As a young woman Zora had a number of jobs and saved up enough money to enrol at Howard University in 1918. There she published her first story. By 1925 Zora had won awards for writing and had caught the attention of prominent black authors living in Harlem. That year she moved to New York and continued her studies, becoming the first black graduate of the all-women's Barnard College. She worked alongside famous creatives including Langston Hughes, Countee Cullen and Alain Locke, who were involved in the black artistic movement known as the Harlem Renaissance. They were called 'the New Negroes'. Zora was celebrated as a writer who personified the movement, and was given the nickname Queen of the Renaissance.

Zora recognized the need to record African American stories, and she celebrated them long before others realized how important they would be. Her famous works include her masterpiece *Their Eyes Were Watching God*, a novel inspired by her Eatonville past. In *Mules and Men*, a collection of stories from north Florida, she tracked and recorded the tales that built up the rich culture of the African American South. *Tell My Horse* was the result of years of research and study of folklore and religion in Jamaica and Haiti. Upon her passing, the famous writer Alice Walker called her 'a Genius of the South'.

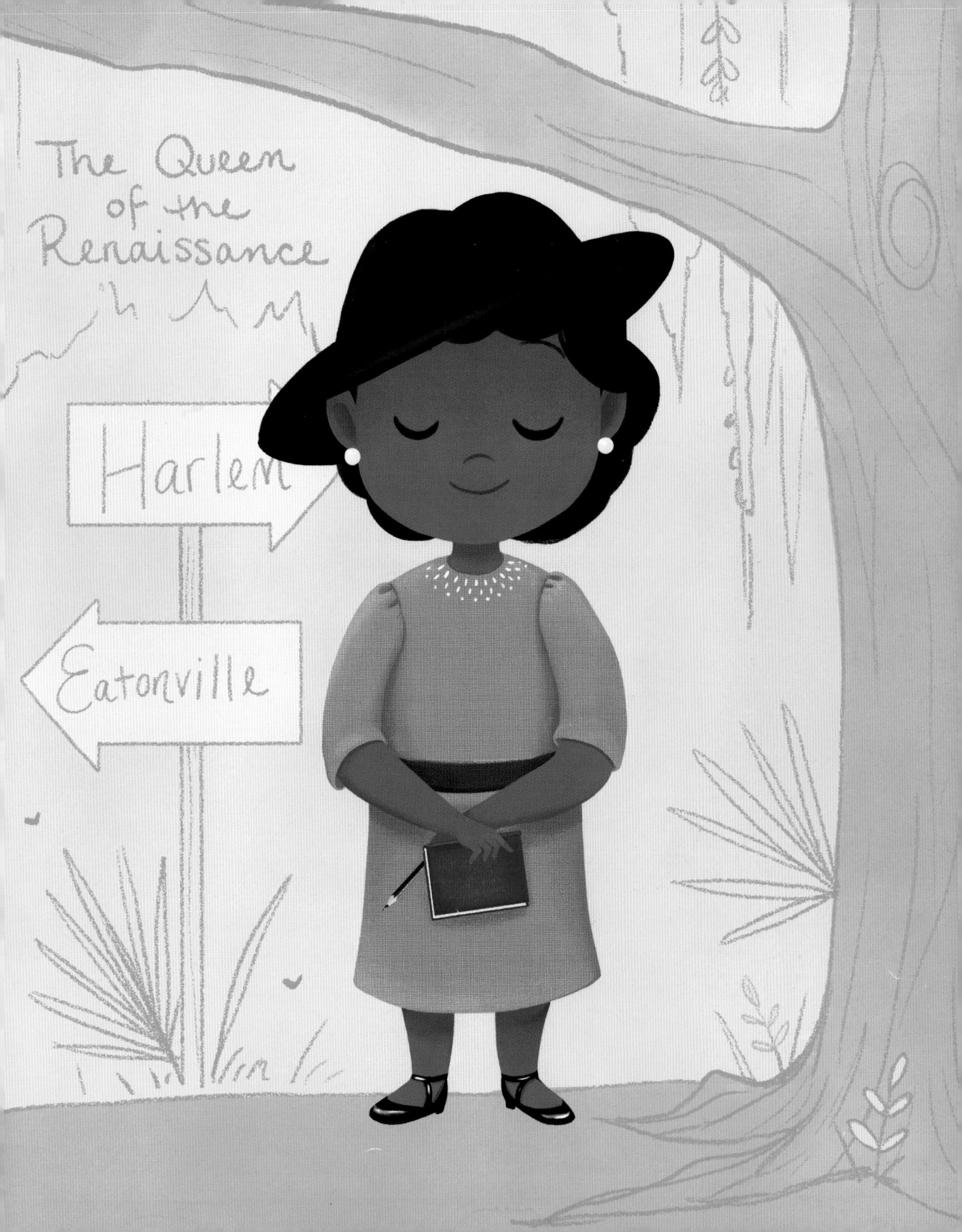
The Queen of the Renaissance
Harlem
Eatonville

Alma Woodsey Thomas
1891–1978

TEACHER, PAINTER

Born in Columbus, Georgia, Alma grew up in a home surrounded by lush landscapes and beautiful plants. In her youth, Alma showed promise in architecture, but was truly in love with art. She said that when she walked into her first art classroom in high school it felt like entering heaven.

She enjoyed working with children and pursued a career as a nursery school teacher. She taught art for several years before attending Howard University. She was the first student in Howard's brand-new art department, whose founder encouraged her to paint full-time. Upon graduation, though, she returned to her first love – education. She devoted her life to children, teaching at Shaw Junior High School for thirty-six years.

She continued painting, and pursued her master's degree in art education at Columbia University in New York City during her summers off. She is most often associated with the group of artists belonging to the Color Field movement – painters who worked only with large shapes, or 'fields' of colour to express themselves.

When she retired from teaching in 1960, Alma concentrated on painting full-time. She had a big art show at Howard University, for which she produced something totally different from anything she had done before. Inspired by nature, she created paintings with tiny bright rectangles and repeating shapes. It became her signature style.

In 1972, when she was eighty years old, Alma's paintings were exhibited at the Whitney Museum of American Art. This was the first-ever solo exhibition of an African American woman artist at one of America's most important art museums. Alma showed the importance of being dedicated to the thing you love and having the patience to let it grow.

"Colour is life."

Alice Ball
1892–1916

CHEMIST, MEDICAL RESEARCHER

Alice's mother and grandfather were both photographers, and as a child she became interested in the chemicals used in photography. She went to college in her home town of Seattle and earned not one but two degrees, in pharmaceutical chemistry and pharmacy. What an accomplishment for a young woman! At the time, most of the African American population in the city was employed in service professions – cleaning homes or preparing food, for example. But Alice defied expectations and her circumstances by seeking an education and a career in science.

In 1915 Alice became the first woman and the first African American to graduate with a master's degree from the University of Hawaii. While working on her thesis, she developed what would become the leading treatment for leprosy, a serious, incurable disease. She found a way for oil from the seed of the chaulmoogra tree to be absorbed into the bloodstream. This treatment became the primary method that would be used until the 1940s, but for a long time no one knew that Alice was the inventor. Less than two years after this discovery, Alice died, and the director of her programme took credit for her findings. Alice's method became known as the Dean Method.

It wasn't until the 1970s that historians unearthed the truth and worked to ensure that Alice got credit for her important discovery. On 29 February 2000 the University of Hawaii recognized her for her work and put up a plaque for her on the only chaulmoogra tree on the school's campus. That day the lieutenant governor of Hawaii declared 29 February Alice Ball Day.

HYDNOCARPUS
WIGHTIANUS
CHAULMOOGRA
ALICE BALL

Bessie Coleman
1892–1926

PILOT

Bessie grew up in a small, segregated town in Texas. At home, with three younger siblings around, she had a lot of responsibilities – washing clothes by hand, fetching clean water – on top of walking four miles to school and back every day.

Bessie knew that one day she would leave her small town. In 1915 she moved to Chicago to live with her older brothers. Returning from the First World War they told her all about being in France and about how the women there could fly planes – unlike the women in America. This got Bessie curious – furiously curious.

She applied to every flying school she could find but was denied entry. No one at any of these schools thought a girl could fly – especially not a black girl. Bessie wanted to prove them wrong. In 1920 she moved to France, where she could finally learn to fly. She was so gifted, she graduated from the ten-month course in only seven months. So in 1921 Bessie became the first African American woman in the world to receive her pilot's licence. She specialized in stunt flying, parachuting and aerial tricks!

After returning home to the United States, Bessie flew for huge crowds. She was very popular among both white and black Americans and stood up against segregation and discrimination whenever she could. She hoped to open up her own flying school for other girls of colour. Unfortunately, during a test flight in 1926 a mechanical issue caused her plane to crash. Bessie passed away, but her legacy lives on. In 1977 the Bessie Coleman Aviators Club opened in Chicago to help women of all races fulfil their dreams of flying.

"I made up my mind to try. I tried and I was successful."

Augusta Savage
1892–1962

EDUCATOR, SCULPTOR

Augusta grew up in a poor family with thirteen brothers and sisters in Green Cove Springs, Florida. As a child, she had no toys to play with, but she loved making things. Augusta spent time in her back garden, where the soil was rich with natural red clay. This was where she learned to make miniature animals. However, her father did not approve of her creativity. Even though it meant angering him, Augusta continued to sculpt.

In 1921 she moved to Harlem, a prominent African American neighbourhood in New York City. At the time, the community was experiencing an exciting boom in the arts known as the Harlem Renaissance, and Augusta was a part of it. She thrived artistically, but this did not change the hardships brought about by the racism that was still common in the United States and around the world. Augusta openly fought racial prejudice in the art world and was labelled a troublemaker. She said that she was standing up not only for herself but for future students of colour.

Augusta dedicated much of her life to teaching and encouraging young people to pursue their artistic passion. She felt that their creations could be part of her legacy. In Harlem she opened her own school – the Savage School of Arts and Crafts – and she became the first director of the Harlem Community Art Center. In 1939 she created her most iconic work: a large piece commissioned by the New York World's Fair entitled *Lift Every Voice and Sing*, also known as *The Harp*. Despite her artistic success, Augusta struggled with finances and racism until late in life, but she always found a way to keep creating art.

Josephine Baker
1906–1975

SINGER, DANCER

Josephine had an early start in the entertainment business. As a child in St Louis, Missouri, she put on song-and-dance shows with the neighbourhood children. By the time she was fourteen she was working as a stagehand at local theatres.

The first time she performed onstage, she made waves with her wild dancing and silliness. She stood out from the chorus line, and the other performers sourly called her a 'scene stealer'. But that was just Josephine's style.

Josephine's career really took off when she went to Europe. France became her adoptive country, and Paris her stage. When she returned to the United States, American audiences were not very receptive to a black woman who seemed too uppity for her own skin. Josephine, meanwhile, was shocked by the prejudice and discrimination she encountered. From then on she insisted on performance contracts that did not allow any form of discrimination and fought for integrated audiences.

Her fearlessness did not end there. During the Second World War Josephine worked for the French Résistance, smuggling secret messages in her sheet music and undergarments. After the war, she was awarded two of France's highest military honours.

Josephine built a large, loving family with adopted children from all over the world. She called them the Rainbow Tribe. In 1963, she travelled back to the United States to accompany Dr Martin Luther King Jr on the famous March on Washington for Jobs and Freedom. She was the only woman slated to speak that day.

Josephine was never one to fall in line. She always stood out and made her own way. She was a brave woman who was so much more than just a performer.

Mahalia Jackson
1911 – 1972

GOSPEL SINGER

Born and raised in New Orleans, Louisiana, Mahalia was always surrounded by the sounds of the blues and Mardi Gras. As a child she sang jazz songs by Bessie Smith in her room at night. But Little Halie, as she was called, came from a religious family, and the only music that was acceptable to them was gospel music. She made her singing debut in the choir at the Mount Moriah Baptist Church and blew everyone away with her enormous voice.

Later in life she felt the urge to sing non-religious music, but she had made a promise to herself and her family to sing only gospel, and she stuck to it. She turned down big nightclub shows and lived on very little money. But in 1947 she recorded a single – 'Move On Up a Little Higher' – that sold over two million copies.

She gained a following around the United States and travelled for performances. Her shows drew large crowds from both the black and white communities. Segregation, however, was still the law of the land, and Mahalia struggled with it during and after her performances. When she was on the road, she kept food in her car, just so she wouldn't have to use the 'coloured' section of a restaurant.

At the request of Dr Martin Luther King Jr, Mahalia participated in the Montgomery Bus Boycott, and in 1963 she performed at the March on Washington for Jobs and Freedom, where Reverend King gave his famous 'I Have a Dream' speech. She was on the podium behind him, and when he started to go off script, she encouraged him. 'Tell 'em, Martin,' she shouted, 'tell 'em about the dream!' That most famous part of his speech wasn't planned, but Mahalia knew how powerful his words were, and how important it would be to share them.

Rosa Parks
1913 – 2005

ACTIVIST, WRITER

Growing up in Montgomery, Alabama, Rosa detested the rules of segregation: having to drink from different water fountains or being barred from whites-only restaurants. In the American South, rules on buses were particularly harsh: a black person had to enter through the front door, pay the fare, leave the bus and then get on again through a rear door. Each bus had three sections: a whites-only section at the front, a black section at the back and an overflow section in the middle. If the middle was empty, a black person could sit there. But if one white person wanted to sit in the middle, every black person would have to get up and stand in the back of the bus.

In December 1955, after a long shift at work, Rosa waited for a bus with empty seats, and finally got one with a seat in the overflow section. But when the white section became full, Rosa and others were asked to move. Enough was enough for Rosa. She refused to relinquish her seat. Rosa was arrested and jailed. She used her one phone call to contact her friends at the National Association for the Advancement of Colored People (NAACP).

Rosa was not the first person to fight these laws, and it wasn't even her first time (she had been arrested previously for defying bus rules). But her protest caught the attention of the whole country. Martin Luther King Jr called for a boycott of all public transport in Montgomery. The Montgomery Bus Boycott was a key event of the Civil Rights Movement and set off a chain reaction of protests across the United States. The boycott was ultimately successful. In 1956, the bus system became integrated!

But there was still a long way to go in the fight for civil rights, so Rosa continued to work with the NAACP and the Black Power Movement throughout her life, and was recognized as the mother of the modern day civil rights movement.

Gwendolyn Brooks
1917–2000

WRITER, POET

Gwendolyn always had a true love of language. She had published her first poem by the age of thirteen, and at sixteen she got the chance to meet famous black writers James Weldon Johnson and Langston Hughes, who both encouraged her writing. Johnson became a mentor to her and urged her to read other poets such as T. S. Eliot and Ezra Pound. Gwendolyn made a name for herself as a writer who focused on the black experience and highlighted the lives of ordinary black folks.

In 1945 she published her first collection of poems about black life, entitled *A Street in Bronzeville*, which earned her significant critical acclaim. In 1949 she wrote another collection of poems, about the coming of age of a young black woman called *Annie Allen*. In 1950 it was awarded the Pulitzer Prize, the most distinguished literary honour in the country. This made Gwendolyn the first African American woman to win the award. She loved the magic that different writing techniques could produce, so all her technical skills were put to use. It was a unique piece of writing with complex wordplay and a creative structure. She focused on small everyday problems to illuminate larger issues and themes, such as a woman's role in society.

In the 1960s she was influenced by a group of young writers who had a strong desire to write poems for black people, by black people, and about black people. This affected her style, which soon became sparser and less technical. Gwendolyn's writing was always a reflection of the times and the world around her and, most important, a reflection of the African American experience.

Ella Fitzgerald
1917 – 1996

JAZZ SINGER

As a young woman in Virginia, Ella longed for independence and dreamed of one day becoming an entertainer – but she was living on the streets and singing for pennies. However, in 1934, at the age of seventeen, she got her big break. She entered the amateur night contest at the Apollo Theater in Harlem. She signed up as a dancer but changed to singing when she saw her competition: they were dressed in sparkling matching dresses, while she was in tattered clothes. But she wowed the audience with her unique voice and won a first prize of $25 (worth about $500 today), literally going from rags to riches.

The following year she landed a role as lead singer with Chick Webb and His Orchestra, a popular band that regularly played at one of Harlem's hottest nightclubs, the Savoy Ballroom. At the same time she was building a solo career. In 1938, she recorded her first album and her first hit single, 'A-Tisket, A-Tasket'. Her career snowballed from there. In the 1950s she developed her famous instrumental style of singing called 'scatting'. She collaborated with greats from all over the music industry, including Duke Ellington, Louis Armstrong, Count Basie and Frank Sinatra. In 1958 she made history when she became the first African American woman to win a Grammy – the recording industry's most prestigious award.

Over her long and successful career she recorded more than two hundred albums and some two thousand songs. Ella has gone down in history as one of the most iconic voices of all time. She was fondly known as the First Lady of Jazz and the First Lady of Song.

THE FIRST LADY OF JAZZ
APOLLO
CLUB
HARLEM
AZZ
A-TISKE
A-TASKE
Ella
Fitz

Mamie Phipps Clark
1917 – 1983

SOCIAL PSYCHOLOGIST, COUNSELLOR

Despite growing up during the Great Depression and living in the segregated South, Mamie had a happy childhood, comforted by family and school. At sixteen she was awarded a scholarship to Howard University. Although she began studying maths and physics, she eventually switched to psychology, like Kenneth Clark, her future husband and research partner.

Mamie had never dreamed that segregation could be challenged, but in the summer of 1938 she worked for civil rights activist and NAACP lawyer Charles Houston. She saw famous lawyers gear up to tackle segregation, and she realized that, with the combined efforts of determined people, they could make real change.

The work Mamie did in college was the beginning of breakthrough research that became known as the 'doll tests'. The studies showed an overwhelming preference for white dolls in black children aged three to seven. The children, half of whom attended segregated schools, were presented with four dolls – two brown with black hair and two white with yellow hair – and were given instructions like, 'Give me the doll that is a nice doll', 'Give me the doll that looks bad', and 'Give me the doll that looks like you'. Mamie and Kenneth concluded that the students from segregated schools had developed a sense of inferiority and self-hatred, and that integration helped both black and white children identify themselves with positivity and improved race relations. This became key evidence in the Supreme Court case Brown v. Board of Education, which, in 1954, ruled racial segregation unconstitutional in American schools.

Mamie's research altered the course of history for every child in America! She followed her passion, and it led her to make a difference in the world.

Katherine Johnson
1918 –

NASA MATHEMATICIAN

Judging by the way Katherine took to maths, you would think it was her first language. As a child, she counted everything. She skipped seven years and graduated ahead of her older siblings. She became a maths teacher, but her mentor at the University of West Virginia encouraged her to pursue a career as a research mathematician. In 1953 Katherine got her chance. NASA's Langley Research Center in Hampton, Virginia, had recently opened a lab that hired African American mathematicians. In a time before there were digital calculators, mobile phones or computer machines, the women and men who performed computations were called 'computers'.

Katherine's first assignment was to the flight research division. The United States was in the middle of the 'space race'; in the 1950s and 60s America and Russia were competing for technological advancement in spaceflight. The top goal: to get a man on the moon. Katherine was one of the people who helped make it happen. Her job was to calculate the flight path for the first mission in space. Imagine: the earth is rotating, the moon is revolving, and a rocket has to follow a very specific trajectory in order to reach its moving target.

Even when mechanical computers were introduced, Katherine was still crucial. She continued computing at NASA until her retirement in 1986, and her work influenced every major space programme up to that point. During the *Friendship 7* mission in 1962, John Glenn, the first American to orbit the earth, refused to launch without verification that Katherine herself had double-checked the maths. In 2015 President Barack Obama awarded Katherine the Presidential Medal of Freedom, America's highest civilian honour.

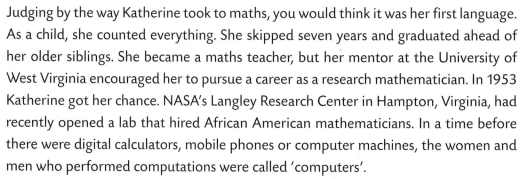

Shirley Chisholm
1924 – 2005

TEACHER, POLITICIAN, ACTIVIST

Shirley was born in Brooklyn, New York, but spent seven years of her childhood in Barbados with her grandmother. When she returned to the United States, she arrived with a new accent and a new sense of boldness others later described as uniquely Caribbean. In college, she became involved in politics and student organizations. She had strong opinions and a fiery determination that made people stop and listen.

Shirley worked as a teacher in Brooklyn and made a name for herself as a leader and advocate in her neighbourhood. She volunteered and consulted at organizations that supported the community, including the Bureau of Child Welfare, the Brooklyn Home for Aged Colored People, and the local NAACP. She was also active in local political organizations such as the Democratic Women's Workshop, the League of Women Voters and the Bedford-Stuyvesant Political League. She stood up for racial equality and welfare, and confronted local politicians. Her outspokenness made her very appealing to the community – and very intimidating to politicians in power.

In 1964 she earned a seat in the New York State Assembly, and in 1968 she became the first black woman elected to the US Congress. She made waves when she crossed party lines and stood up to the old leaders of her party. She was an independent thinker and was never one to stay in her own lane. In 1972 she announced she would be running for president, making history as the first woman and first person of colour to bid for a major party nomination. She ultimately lost, but she did achieve her goal of making her party more aware of and responsive to the people.

"I am the candidate of the people".

Althea Gibson
1927–2003

TENNIS CHAMPION

A self-described 'street rebel', Althea was a child with a lot of energy. Growing up on the streets of Harlem, she preferred to play pool, go boxing and bowling, or play basketball or stickball rather than do her homework. She struggled with rules, but everything changed when, at the age of fourteen, she found tennis. Members of the Harlem Cosmopolitan Club noticed her talent and took her under their wings, teaching her the game and a respect for the rules.

Once she committed herself to the sport, she was a force to be reckoned with! By the age of fifteen she had won her first American Tennis Association National Junior Championship. Most sports were segregated at the time, so when Althea became the first black athlete to enter a US national competition, it was a milestone. Althea became the first black tennis player to compete at the US National Championships in 1950, and then was the first black player at Wimbledon in 1951. Her 1956 victory at the French Open made her the first African American to win a Grand Slam. Her wins paved the way for black tennis players to come, including Venus and Serena Williams. Despite the barriers she broke in the public eye, segregation still kept her from entering through the front door, eating with the other players and using the locker rooms.

In 1958 she retired from tennis. In those days it was difficult to make a living playing sport. Even though she was regarded as one of the best athletes in the world, Althea had to return to the real world and find work. But she wasn't finished with being a rebel: later in life she started playing golf and became the first black woman to compete on the professional tour.

Maya Angelou
1928–2014

POET, ACTIVIST

Maya was known as a writer and poet, but she was so much more. During her long life she would take on many roles: film-maker, dancer, singer, actor, activist, editor, Grammy winner, cable-car operator, playwright, author and legend.

Long before she found success, she was just a little girl trying to find her voice. Born Marguerite Annie Johnson, she spent much of her childhood living with her grandmother in the small segregated town of Stamps, Arkansas. Her only companion was her older brother, who gave her the nickname Maya.

Maya experienced abuse when she was only eight years old. The fear and trauma it left behind were enough to convince her never to speak again. For five years Maya did not utter a word to anyone. But during those five years, she read. She devoured every book in the black school library, and every book she could get her hands on from the white school library. It wasn't until a childhood mentor challenged her, saying, 'You don't really love poetry unless you speak it', that Maya spoke again.

She was a master wordsmith who approached language with thoughtfulness and patience. Another challenge sparked her writing career. When her editor told her 'It's nearly impossible to write a lyrical autobiography', Maya went on to write her bestselling masterpiece *I Know Why the Caged Bird Sings*, a lyrical and poetic telling of her childhood.

In 1993 she became the first female poet to write and recite a poem for the presidential inauguration, which brought her poetry into the mainstream again. Maya Angelou did so much in her lifetime and inspired everyone around her.

Nichelle Nichols
1932 –

ACTRESS, SINGER

In her youth, Nichelle was a gifted dancer, actor and singer. She got her first professional acting role when she was only fourteen, and had a successful theatrical career for several years. In 1966 Nichelle landed the role with which she would make her mark on the world. She was cast in the brand-new science fiction series *Star Trek*, as communications officer Lieutenant Uhura, becoming the first woman of colour in history in a leading role on a prime-time television show. Uhura was smart, brave and dignified, and treated with respect. It was truly a groundbreaking role, considering that in those days people of colour were usually cast as servants.

In 1968, at the height of the Civil Rights Movement, Nichelle and one of her white cast mates made waves when their characters shared a shocking on-screen interracial kiss. Many Americans were angered by the display of integration on a national television show, and the studio received letters of complaint. Producers responded by cutting Nichelle's lines, making her scenes shorter, and relegating her to the background.

She considered returning to stage acting. But a chance encounter with Dr Martin Luther King Jr changed her mind. Dr King, a self-proclaimed 'Trekkie', urged Nichelle to stay on the show because she was a symbol of hope and a source of inspiration to people of colour across America. This would prove to be exactly right: Dr Mae Jemison names Nichelle as her inspiration to apply to NASA – and she went on to be the first African American woman in space!

After *Star Trek* Nichelle continued to inspire people. She worked for NASA, travelling around the United States to recruit young men and women of colour.

Nina Simone
1933 – 2003

PIANIST, SINGER, ACTIVIST

Nina – born Eunice Waymon – grew up in a home where music was all around. A prodigy with a love for Bach, Beethoven and Brahms, she dreamed of becoming the first black concert pianist.

Activism, however, was as much a part of her as her music was. At the age of twelve, when Eunice's parents were removed from the front row of one of her recitals to make room for a white couple, she stood up and refused to play until the injustice was corrected. The event left her hardened and distrustful but demonstrated the power of activism through music.

As a young adult, financial troubles and discrimination got in the way of her studies, so Eunice began giving piano lessons. She soon learned that she could earn double the money by performing in nightclubs in Atlantic City. When nightclub owners informed her that playing the piano was not enough, she had to become a singer. She took the name Nina Simone and began to sing. Was there any way of knowing then that hers would become one of the most iconic voices in the history of music?

Onstage, her musical genius really showed. She combined different musical styles, and played a very wide range of music. She mixed jazz, folk music and blues, and always had a soft spot for classical piano. Nina used her music to stand up for social justice, writing songs in response to the assassination of Civil Rights leader Medgar Evers and the Birmingham church bombing. She became a leading voice in the Civil Rights Movement while her songs served as its soundtrack.

Audre Lorde
1934–1992

POET, ESSAYIST, ACTIVIST

Ever since her childhood, Audre had loved reading and writing. She wrote her first poem at the age of eight, and while she was still at school her work was published in *Seventeen* magazine. After graduating Audre took a trip to Mexico that she found eye-opening. There she found a place where her race was not something to be ashamed of. Seeing this made her realize that she had let that shame keep her silent. She learned just how important her voice was, and began to use it.

She returned to the United States with a newfound confidence and studied for a degree in library science. She graduated and worked as a librarian, but Audre did not sit quietly. Her voice was her new instrument, which she used to speak up and speak out. The Civil Rights Movement was building steam, and Audre was an active member. She soon became a prominent and vocal leader, activist and feminist, and worked alongside other famous writers such as Nikki Giovanni and Amiri Baraka. Among her famous works is her book of poetry *From a Land Where Other People Live*.

At the age of forty-four Audre was diagnosed with breast cancer. Instead of taking the news quietly, she began speaking openly about it. She wrote *The Cancer Journals*, documenting her surgeries and experiences. It opened up a conversation about a subject that had rarely been talked about. When she was fifty, the cancer spread to her liver. She wrote and spoke about the journey to find new treatment, she exposed and criticized the medical institutions and their insensitive practices, and she shared her experiences with others. Audre is remembered as an outspoken leader and a fierce advocate for those without a voice.

Raven Wilkinson
1935 –

BALLERINA

Raven's love for dance began at the age of five, when her mother took her to a performance by the Ballet Russe de Monte Carlo. Fifteen years later she made history by becoming their first full-time African American dancer. It was a difficult journey. The life of a ballerina is never easy, but Raven also faced prejudice and discrimination because of her race.

The Ballet Russe toured through the segregated South, and it was risky to have an integrated cast. Friends warned her that they would never take her because she was black. Her talent was undeniable, though, and in 1955 Raven was accepted on a trial basis. She was fair-skinned, so she was encouraged to wear white make-up. She kept her race a secret but refused to lie about it when she was asked outright.

Even though she had a successful two years with the Ballet Russe, racism restricted her career. Exhausted and heartbroken, she left dance for a while. In 1967 she was invited to join the Dutch National Ballet and moved to Holland for six years. As she was nearing the age of forty, she believed that her dancing career was over, so she retired and moved back to the United States. Almost immediately she received a call from the ballet master at the New York City Opera, and was asked to dance with them at Lincoln Center. Raven danced until she was fifty and continued acting in the opera until 2011.

Every step of the way was a challenge, but Raven persisted. Her strength and grace led the way for dancers such as Misty Copeland to take on the role of principal dancer at the American Ballet Theatre and defy long-standing beauty and body standards for ballerinas.

SINGER

From a young age Shirley's big voice was unmistakable. She did not always find encouragement at school, but she was certainly praised by her family, from whom she got her singing talent and strong will. But life was not easy at home. Born in Cardiff, Wales, the youngest of seven children in a blended mixed-race family, times were always tough. Racial discrimination was a constant issue, and Shirley's family struggled with extreme poverty. Getting food on the table was a daily concern and Shirley had to leave school at the age of sixteen to start work in a factory. Still passionate about music, she continued to sing in her spare time, performing at pubs and clubs after work and at weekends. It was only a matter of time before her big voice got her noticed.

At nineteen she was discovered by her soon-to-be manager, Michael Sullivan. Together they developed her signature glamorous look and she released her first few singles. Shirley's big break came in 1964 when she recorded the title track for the James Bond film, *Goldfinger*. Her booming voice filled cinemas all over the world during the opening credits of one of the year's biggest movies. It launched her on the international stage and her voice became forever linked with one of the most famous Bond films.

She went on to sing the title tracks for other Bond films – *Diamonds Are Forever* and *Moonraker*. These landmark songs, along with her singles 'Big Spender' and 'I Am What I Am', helped to establish her career and her glamorous vibe. She was the voice of Bond and became synonymous with cool and elegance.

In 2000 she was made a Dame Commander of the Order of the British Empire for her contribution to the arts. In her career she has sold over 135 million records and she will go down in history as one of the world's most iconic singers.

Wilma Rudolph
1940–1994

SPRINTER

Wilma is one of America's most famous sprinters, but her journey to the finish line was a long one. When she was four years old, Wilma contracted polio, for which there was no cure at the time. The disease paralysed her left leg, and she was forced to wear a metal leg brace.

Wilma was different and got teased a lot. She was small, and her sandy-coloured hair made her stand out. But she was also strong. With lots of hard work, determination and physical therapy, she was walking without her brace by the age of twelve. A year later she was running faster than all the boys and girls in her class.

Soon she had joined track-and-field and was winning every event! When she was only sixteen years old, she earned her first Olympic medal at the 1956 games in Melbourne, Australia. Only a few years before, she had never even heard of the Olympic Games, but now Wilma was determined to win gold.

In Rome in 1960 she became the first American woman to win *three* gold medals in a single Olympics. When she returned home to Clarksville, Tennessee, there was a parade in her honour. But Wilma found out that the organizers had planned a segregated event, so she refused to participate until they agreed to integrate it. As an American icon, Wilma knew that her stance on civil rights could have an impact. She didn't let the fact that she was so young stop her. How amazing that one brave voice can make a difference!

Wilma later became a teacher and coach. In 1981 she started the Wilma Rudolph Foundation to support young athletes.

Bonita Mabo
Circa 1943–

ACTIVIST

Although Bonita spent a happy childhood growing up in a close-knit community of South Sea Islanders near Townsville, she longed to know her native land. Her grandmother was originally from the Aboriginal community on Palm Island and her grandfather from Tanna Island near Vanuatu. Both were kidnapped, taken to Queensland, Australia, and forced to work on the sugar plantations – a practice known as 'blackbirding'. This is part of a long history of displacement and strife between Australia's First Peoples and the British colonizers. Bonita spent much of her life campaigning on behalf of indigenous Australians and standing up for the rights of her own people.

She worked alongside her famous activist husband Eddie Mabo. While he was passionate about protecting the land rights of his people, the Torres Straits Islanders, Bonita fought for quality education for the indigenous community. Together they had ten children, but Eddie was often away, and Bonita essentially raised them on her own. Unhappy with the education they were receiving in the school system in Queensland, Bonita took action. In 1973 she and Eddie opened the Black Community School in Townsville – Australia's first Aboriginal community school.

After her husband's death in 1992 Bonita began to campaign on behalf of the South Sea Islanders. She wanted them to be recognized as a distinct ethnic group, and their culture to be celebrated. In 2013 she was honoured as Officer in the Order of Australia for her work as an advocate and community leader for the Aboriginals, the Torres Strait Islanders and the South Sea Islanders. She gave her people a voice and dedicated her life to fighting for their rights.

Angela Davis
1944–

ACTIVIST, SCHOLAR

Angela grew up in racially segregated Birmingham, Alabama, a city at the centre of the fight for civil rights. By the time she was a teenager Angela was already actively involved in the movement. She organized interracial study groups, which were broken up by the police. This was only the beginning for Angela's passion for activism and scholarship.

At college she studied philosophy under a famous German thinker named Herbert Marcuse. She says he taught her that she could be an academic and a scholar as well as an activist and a revolutionary.

Angela was always outspoken. She was linked to the Black Panther Party, as well as a member of and later president of the Communist Party USA. Both groups were considered dangerous because of their opposition to the US government, so she was put on the Federal Bureau of Investigation's 'most wanted' list. Her major passions included fighting for prison reform and against police brutality. She was labelled a troublemaker for fighting the system. She lost her teaching job at the University of California, Los Angeles (UCLA), but responded by bringing a legal case against them. She was put in prison for conspiracy charges, but was acquitted sixteen months later. Angela Davis is revered for fighting back against systems of oppression, but through all this she was devoted to teaching, and remained a professor of philosophy into her seventies.

"I am no longer accepting the things I cannot change. I am changing the things I cannot accept."

Octavia E. Butler
1947–2006

WRITER

Despite her struggle with dyslexia, Octavia began writing when she was ten years old. One day she was watching a bad science-fiction movie on TV and was inspired to write something better. This was her first attempt at writing sci-fi – a genre that would become synonymous with her name. She continued to write short stories through college and attended Pennsylvania's renowned Clarion Science Fiction Writers Workshop.

In 1976 she published her first novel, *Patternmaster*. It made waves: a science-fiction novel with black female characters had never been seen before. However, Octavia's big moment came in 1979, when she published *Kindred*. Inspired by her mother's experiences as a maid, it tells the story of a black woman who travels back to the times of slavery. She wanted to write a story 'that would make others feel the history: the pain and fear that black people have had to live through in order to endure'.

Octavia's publishers had a hard time categorizing her books, especially *Kindred*. Was it fantasy, history, science fiction or fiction? And they were unsure about her audience: did black women read sci-fi? Octavia and her books proved that they did!

Octavia created a space for black girls to like science fiction – a genre historically associated with white male writers and readers. She wanted to change the industry's perception of who the writers *and* the readers were and show that science fiction could be for anyone. Through her fantastical works, Octavia discussed important topics in her own life and society: race, slavery, humanity and religion. In 1995 she was awarded the important MacArthur Foundation Fellowship – the first science-fiction writer to receive it.

Julie Dash
1952 –

FILMMAKER

It seems that Julie always knew she wanted to be a filmmaker, but her journey began with some luck. As a teenager she participated in a film workshop at the Studio Museum in Harlem. She thought it was for still photography, but to her surprise it was for motion pictures – and the medium stuck. She went on to study film, did a two-year fellowship at the American Film Institute, and then got her master of fine arts degree at the University of California, Los Angeles (UCLA).

During her time at UCLA she joined a new generation of black students on the directing course. All of them were fuelled by a love of cinema and a drive to make new, inclusive work. They were known as the filmmakers of the LA Rebellion. They all collaborated and helped each other out – and Julie was the best at doing hair and make-up!

In 1991 Julie made her first feature-length film, *Daughters of the Dust*, about a family from the Gullah/Geechee community – descendants of African slaves living off the South Carolina/Georgia coast. The film is a lyrical family drama about three generations of women and their religious and traditional preparations for a move north. This was the first film by an African American woman to receive a general theatrical release in the United States. In 2004 the Library of Congress placed *Daughters of the Dust* on the National Film Registry – a list of distinguished films preserved as national treasures.

Julie's passion for film is truly remarkable. She participated in many distinguished programmes and has been nominated for countless awards and honours. In an industry dominated by men, she was often the first wherever she went, but she would definitely not be the last.

Diane Abbott
1953 –

POLITICIAN

Growing up, Diane was something of an outsider. The only black student at the Harrow County Grammar School for Girls, Diane was fiercely independent. Unhappy with her progress at school, Diane studied at her own rate and won top marks, but her boldness did not gain her teachers' support even when she was accepted at Cambridge University. Despite her teachers, her parents were always supportive. They knew that she would have to be twice as good as the other students to succeed.

Diane studied History at Newnham College, Cambridge. Class divisions set her apart from the other students and she was often lonely. Diane thinks of this time as character-building and she did not let it stop her from helping people. After graduating she worked as a civil servant, served on the National Council for Civil Liberties and was a reporter for Thames Television. Always looking for a way to make real change in the world, Diane turned to politics. A long-time member of the Labour Party, Diane first ran for office in 1982 when she served on Westminster City Council. In 1987 she made history when she became the first black woman elected to Parliament, representing Hackney North and Stoke Newington.

As an MP, Diane has been passionate about fighting for human rights and civil liberties. Always dedicated to her party, she has taken on many roles, including shadow secretary of state for public health and shadow home secretary. She continues to serve and was re-elected in 2017. Race and class discrimination were hurdles Diane had to face along the way, but with her determination and her passion for public service she has made her mark.

Ruby Bridges
1954 –

ACTIVIST

Ruby made history in 1960 when, at the age of six, she became the first student to attend an all-white school in New Orleans. Although some other cities had already begun to desegregate (a Supreme Court ruling in 1954 declared that 'separate but equal' was in fact not equal), there were some cities where schools were still divided by colour. But after an important ruling, the court ordered the schools in New Orleans to be desegregated, and Ruby was selected to be the first black student to attend William Frantz Elementary School.

Every step of the way was a challenge. Long before her first day, Ruby had to take an exam just to gain admission to the school – one that was written in such a way that black students were less likely to pass. Her father feared what it might mean if she passed, but her mother pushed for Ruby to have a better education.

Many people did not support desegregation, and on Ruby's first day protesters surrounded the school. Ruby had to be escorted by her mother and US marshals in order to enter. At her age, it was hard for her to grasp what was going on. Many years later, she said she thought it was a Mardi Gras celebration because of the number of people out on the streets. She had no idea that they were there to protest against her enrolment.

Once she was inside the school, the difficulties continued. White parents withdrew their children, and many of the teachers refused to teach a black student. Only one person agreed to teach her: a young woman who had recently moved to Louisiana from Boston. Miss Henry became Ruby's only confidante and friend.

During the fight for civil rights, Ruby became a symbol of the vulnerability of all black Americans.

William Frantz Elementary
1 x 2 = 2
2 x 2 = 4
3 x 2 = 6
4 x 2 = 8
5 x 2 = 10
6 x 2 = 12
Miss He
September

Oprah Winfrey
1954–

BROADCAST JOURNALIST, MEDIA MOGUL

From an early age Oprah had a talent for speaking. The future queen of daytime television was reciting poems by the time she was three. After a childhood marked by abuse and neglect, during her teens she moved in with her father, who encouraged her to read books and focus on her education.

While she was still at school in Nashville, Tennessee, she got a radio job and then moved to local television news, eventually becoming a news anchor (while still in college!). She hit a rough patch when she was demoted for getting too emotionally involved in her news stories, but soon found her home in talk shows, where her compassion and empathy were an asset and her dynamic personality was unmistakable. In 1985 she transformed a Chicago-area show into *The Oprah Winfrey Show*, and a year later it was broadcast nationally. In 1986 she started her own production company, Harpo Productions, and became the first woman of colour in history to own and produce her own television show.

Oprah's career did not stop at television. She has produced movies and plays, and launched her own television network and a magazine. She has written books and created the hugely influential Oprah's Book Club. She has won countless awards, and was the first black female billionaire in the US.

Oprah consistently uses her influence to help others. Through her various charities she provides funds for schools, communities and families in need, and vulnerable young women and children all over the world. In 2013 President Barack Obama awarded her the highest civilian honour – the Presidential Medal of Freedom. Despite the hardships of her past she used her gifts to build a strong career for herself, and created a platform to effect real change in the world.

Dr Mae Jemison
1956 –

ENGINEER, PHYSICIAN, ASTRONAUT

As a child Mae loved reading, especially books about science and astronomy. By the time she was in nursery school she knew she wanted to become a scientist. This, however, did not keep her from other passions. Mae also wanted to be a dancer, and throughout her youth she studied every type of dance.

In the 1970s Mae read chemical engineering and African American studies. When she learned about Dr Martin Luther King Jr, she saw his work as a call to action to help people, so after graduating she decided to become a doctor.

She joined the Peace Corps in 1983, and travelled to West Africa on a two-year programme to provide medical assistance to those in need. After returning, she saw major changes taking place at NASA. In 1983, for example, Sally Ride became the first American woman in space. Mae had always imagined herself in space, but hesitated to pursue that dream. But it was seeing the actress Nichelle Nichols play Lieutenant Uhura in the TV show *Star Trek* that finally inspired her to apply to NASA. In 1987 Mae became the first black woman in the astronaut training programme, and a few years later she flew into orbit – as the first African American woman in space.

Mae still wanted to have a direct impact on people, so in 1993 she left NASA and created her own company, the Jemison Group, which researches ways in which technology can help people in their daily lives. She also started the Dorothy Jemison Foundation for Excellence, which in 1994 launched The Earth We Share, a science camp for children.

The first
African American
woman astronaut

Tessa Sanderson
1956–

JAVELIN THROWER, HEPTATHLETE

Born in St Elizabeth, Jamaica, Tessa moved to Britain when she was only nine years old. Swapping the tropical Caribbean for an English city might seem a scary move but, helped by her love of sport, Tessa quickly made Wolverhampton her home. She joined the local club, where she showed a lot of promise in javelin and other heptathlon events. She was a rising star on the field and by the age of sixteen had already won her first javelin championship. Over the next few years she took part in numerous competitions, breaking records all along the way. By 1976 she had earned her spot in her first Olympics Games. Meanwhile she also participated in the Commonwealth Games – in the heptathlon, an event with seven elements (100-metre hurdles, high jump, shot put, 200 metres, long jump, javelin throw and 800 metres), and in 1981 she became the top British woman heptathlete.

Tessa's biggest moment came in 1984, when she won a gold medal for Great Britain at the Olympics in Los Angeles. This made her the first British woman to win Olympic gold in the heptathlon, and the first black British woman to win any Olympic gold. Following her landmark win, in 1985 she was appointed a Member of the Order of the British Empire. In over 20 years of competition Tessa broke both records and barriers. She is only one of five women ever to throw the javelin over 73 metres!

In 1997 she retired from competition but did not give up her passion for sport. She ran the Newham Sports Academy which helped find and train athletes to represent Britain in the 2012 Olympic and Paralympic games. Afterwards she started the Tessa Sanderson Foundation and Academy, a charity that educates abled and disabled young athletes and helps them to achieve their sporting goals.

Florence Joyner
1959–1998

SPRINTER

Florence always loved to stand out – which wasn't easy growing up with ten brothers and sisters. Her mother was a model and her grandmother a beautician, so style and beauty were always a part of her life.

Her athletic talents emerged early on: when visiting her father in the Mojave Desert, she caught a jackrabbit that tried to outrun her. By the age of seven she was already winning races, and she had a successful athletics career at school and college. At California State University, Northridge, she met her longtime coach Bob Kersee.

By 1982 Florence was making a name for herself in the track-and-field world. She stood out as a superb athlete, but her personal style did not go unnoticed. On the track she sported flashy uniforms – often ones that she had designed herself – and long fingernails. In 1984 she participated in her first Olympics and won a silver medal.

She took time off from running for other jobs, including bank representative and beautician. She married fellow runner Al Joyner, whose sister Jackie Joyner soon married Florence's old coach Bob Kersee. With a family full of runners, she was encouraged to get back into competition, so she set her sights on the 1988 Olympics. She won one silver and two gold medals, and set a new world record that she still holds to this day. She also picked up the nickname Flo-Jo.

Even with a successful athletic career, Florence had other passions and interests – she developed a clothing brand and nail products, wrote children's books and established a youth foundation. She would never be defined as one thing, and would most certainly always stand out from the crowd.

Lorna Simpson
1960–

PHOTOGRAPHER

Born in Brooklyn, New York, Lorna began her career as a documentary photographer with the goal of capturing life as it is. After college, though, she took a trip to Europe and Africa and became interested in changing the way people could experience photographs. She wanted to use photography as a way of *understanding* the subject instead of just looking at it. In particular, she wanted to create a better understanding of African American women. Much of Lorna's work focused on experimenting and finding new ways to develop imagery.

In the 1980s, while a post-graduate at the University of California, San Diego, Lorna began to incorporate text into her images to add a second layer of meaning. She called this new style 'photo-text', and these became her most iconic works. She brought attention to contemporary society's relationship with and perception of African American women. Through her art she tackled subjects such as race, gender and identity. Many of her works obscure the figures' faces – she calls them 'anti-portraits'.

Lorna has exhibited her photographs at some of the most respected venues around the art world. In 1990 she became the first African American woman to exhibit at the biggest international arts festival, the Venice Biennale.

Lorna continues to push the boundaries of photography and experiments with other media, such as video, drawing and silk-screen printing. Her work has helped pave the way and create a space in the fine-art world for other black women artists.

More Little Leaders

It was so hard to choose only forty bold women to present in this book that I couldn't help but share a few more with you. Some of these women have followed in the footsteps of those who came before them; others have paved their own way. Dorothy Height opened a door for all women in the Civil Rights Movement, and Carrie Mae Weems helped earn a place at the table for black women artists to follow. Without Zora Neale Hurston, some of Alice Walker's finest essays might never have been written.

See if you can find connections between a few of these Little Leaders and others throughout the book.

FANNY EATON • 1835–1924
A model for Pre-Raphaelite painters, known for her incomparable beauty

MARY JANE PATTERSON • 1840–1894
First black woman in the United States to graduate from university

ADELAIDE HALL • 1901–1993
UK-based jazz singer of the Harlem Renaissance

DOROTHY HEIGHT • 1912–2010
Women's rights activist, godmother of
the American Civil Rights Movement

ALICE WALKER • 1944–
Pulitzer Prize winner for her novel
The Color Purple

OLIVE MORRIS • 1952–1979
Community activist, founder of women's
campaign groups in Brixton, London

CARRIE MAE WEEMS • 1953–
Multimedia artist known for focusing
on African American life

ZADIE SMITH • 1975–
English novelist, essayist and
short-story writer

VENUS WILLIAMS • 1980–
First black woman to be ranked No. 1
since tennis's Open Era began (in 1968)

SERENA WILLIAMS • 1981–
Most Grand Slam wins by a tennis
player in the Open Era

MISTY COPELAND • 1982–
First black principal ballerina at
the American Ballet Theatre

NICOLA ADAMS • 1982–
British professional boxer, the first woman
to win an Olympic boxing gold medal

Further Reading,

WATCHING AND LISTENING

Doing the research for this book was an incredible experience. It was eye-opening and heart-wrenching, but most importantly it made me want to learn more. Sadly, I could not fit as much into these pages as I wanted. It was a difficult task to tell these women's stories in a couple of paragraphs, but I hope I have sparked your interest to learn more. Here are some places to begin.

BOOKS

Olson, Lynne. *Freedom's Daughters: The Unsung Heroines of the Civil Rights Movement from 1830 to 1970.* New York: Scribner, 2002.

Shetterly, Margot Lee. *Hidden Figures Young Readers' Edition.* New York: HarperCollins, 2016.

Warren, Wini. *Black Women Scientists in the United States.* Bloomington: Indiana University Press, 2000.

RECORDINGS

Bassey, Shirley, 'Goldfinger', 1964.

Fitzgerald, Ella, 'A-Tisket, A-Tasket', 1938.

Jackson, Mahalia, 'How I Got Over', 1961.

Simone, Nina, 'To Be Young, Gifted and Black', 1970.

WEBSITES

Archive.org

Biography.com

Brittanica.com

Encyclopedia.com

Makers.org

NAACP.org

NASA.gov

Pulitzer.org

RECOMMENDED BOOKS BY BOLD WOMEN

Sojourner Truth: *Narrative of Sojourner Truth*

Zora Neale Hurston: *Their Eyes Were Watching God*

Gwendolyn Brooks: *A Street in Bronzeville*

Maya Angelou: *I Know Why the Caged Bird Sings*

Nichelle Nichols: *Beyond Uhura: Star Trek and Other Memories*

Audre Lorde: *Zami: A New Spelling of My Name*

Octavia E. Butler: *Kindred*

Oprah Winfrey: *What I Know for Sure*

FILMS AND TV

Dash, Julie, dir. *Daughters of the Dust*. American Playhouse, 1991.

Eyes on the Prize. Fourteen episodes aired from 21 January, 1987, to 5 March, 1990, on PBS.

Hercules, Bob and Rita Coburn Whack, dirs. *Maya Angelou: And Still I Rise*. American Masters, 2017.

Nelson, Stanley, dir. *Freedom Riders*. Aired 16 May, 2011, on PBS.

Glossary

Abolition of Slavery: By 1840 most slaves living in the north of the United States had been set free. Slavery was officially outlawed everywhere in the country in 1865.

African American Civil Rights Movement (Civil Rights Movement): The fight for racial equality in the US that took place during the century following the Civil War. The movement is often associated with protests and action of the 1950s and 1960s, with leaders like Dr Martin Luther King Jr, Malcolm X and Rosa Parks.

American Civil War (1860–1865): The war started when the southern states of America opposed the abolition of slavery and separated from the US. Eventually the North reclaimed the South and slavery was officially outlawed.

Civil Rights: Basic rights that every person has guaranteed under the law.

Confederacy/Southern States: The states that separated from the US during the Civil War, becoming the Confederate States of America, with Jefferson Davis as their president.

Lynching: The act of murder by a mob, usually by hanging. During the nineteenth and twentieth centuries black people were often attacked as punishment for an alleged offence without being given a fair trial.

North/Unionist States: The states in the North that stayed loyal to the US Government.

Segregation: The process by which people in the US were separated by race. Integration or desegregation is the act of bringing people from different races together.

Underground Railroad: The name for the secret network of people, homes and hideouts that slaves in the southern US used to escape to freedom in the North.

Acknowledgements

It has been a dream to bring this book to life with the team from Little, Brown. I feel so lucky to work with such thoughtful, creative, and supportive people, and I am so happy to know my Little Leaders have a home there. My editor, Farrin Jacobs, is an actual magician, and it was beautiful to witness her craft at work. Creative director and designer Dave Caplan is hands down the most thoughtful and thorough creator I've ever worked with. Many thanks to Kheryn Callender and Nicole Brown for their hard work and constant wrangling of my e-mails and uploads, as well as to Erika Schwartz and Jen Graham. A special thank you for the research and guidance from Anna Barnes and Emily Lunn from Penguin Random House UK. Knowing this book was in their care was both reassuring and incredibly humbling.

This entire journey has been uncharted territory for me, but my amazing literary agent, Carrie Hannigan, has been with me every step of the way. Her knowledge and expertise is matched only by her caring and consideration. I have big dreams for these Little Leaders, and Carrie is helping make them into realities.

Thank you to my incredibly supportive friends and family, who lent their ears to my ideas and concerns and participated in my emergency brainstorming sessions: Nicole Harrison, Kassiopia Ragoonanan, Kwesi Johnson, Elizabeth Webb and Lindsey Arturo.

A huge praise-hands emoji is due to the thousands of people on social media who supported these Little Leaders and begged me to keep going. I'd like to thank black women especially: the outpouring of love and messages of appreciation I receive every day are a constant reminder that I come from the most supportive community of people in the world.

And lastly, this book is the product of many, but no two people are as excited for its release and deserving of praise as my parents, Ted and Chandra Harrison. Their love and support is the foundation for its creation. They were champions of the Little Leaders when they were just doodles, and they acted as my advisors, agents, art directors, editors and publicists long before I ever signed any deals. To say they've always supported my artistic career is a vast understatement. They saw possibilities for me even when I had lost sight of them, and for that I am forever grateful.